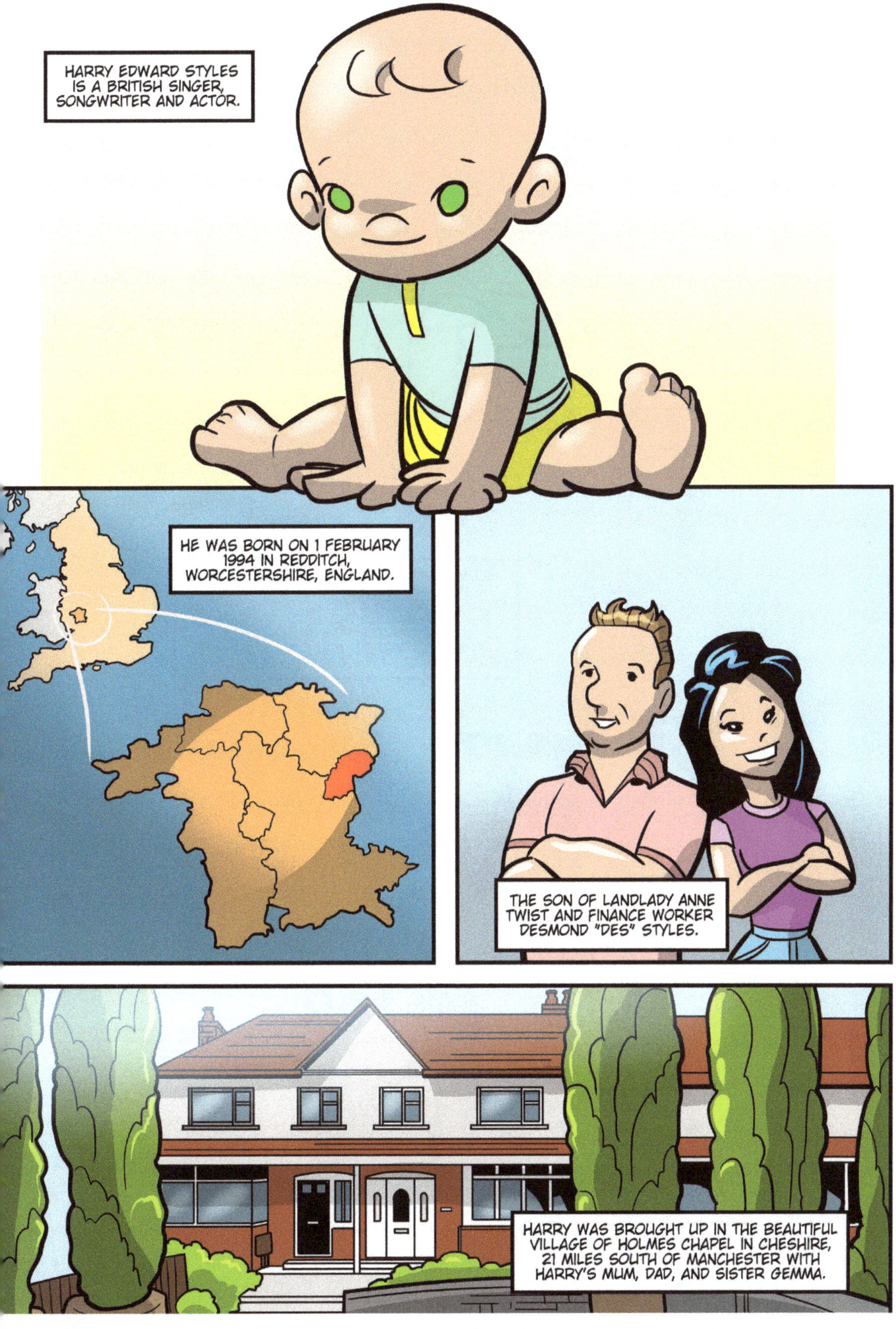

APRIL 24, 2008, STYLES MADE HIS START IN MUSIC WHILE A STUDENT AT HOLMES CHAPEL COMPREHENSIVE SCHOOL IN CHESHIRE, ENGLAND.

HARRY ALWAYS HAD A TASTE FOR MUSIC, WHICH IS WHY HE DECIDED TO GET TOGETHER WITH HIS FRIENDS TO CREATE A BAND CALLED "WHITE ESKIMO".

"WHITE ESKIMO" IS A BRITISH BAND CONSISTING OF STYLES AS THE LEAD VOCALIST WHILE CURRENT FRONT MAN WILL SWEENY PLAYED DRUMS, NICK CLOUGH ON BASS AND HAYDN MORRIS ON GUITAR. HARRY STYLES WAS ONE OF THE ORIGINAL MEMBERS OF THE BAND BEFORE HE LEFT TO AUDITION FOR "THE X FACTOR".

THEY SOON ENTERED THEIR LOCAL BATTLE OF THE BANDS COMPETITION AND WENT TO WIN AT THE EVENT. THIS PROMPTED STYLES TO AUDITION FOR "THE X FACTOR". SOON AFTER CLOUGH AND MORRIS LEFT THE BAND. ALL THREE FORMER MEMBERS WERE REPLACED LATER BY ALEX LEWIS, ROY BENNETT AND BRAD NEVINSON. THE BAND EVENTUALLY WENT TO RELEASE THEIR FIRST EXTENDED PLAY TITLED "100X" IN 2015.-

AUGUST 19, 2011, "WHAT MAKES YOU BEAUTIFUL" IT WAS THE FIRST SONG OF THE BAND WHICH LED TO THEIR DEBUT, CURRENTLY HAS 1,298,869,611 VIEWS ON YOUTUBE.

DECEMBER 18, 2011, HARRY AND THE REST OF THE BAND MEMBERS, STARED THEIR FIRST TOUR, WHICH IS CALLED "UP ALL NIGHT" TOUR.

FEBRUARY 3, 2012, ONE DIRECTION WON ITS FIRST BRIT AWARD FOR BEST BRITISH SINGLE IN 2012 FOR WHAT MAKES YOU BEAUTIFUL. BEHIND THEIR BACKS THEY HAVE A TOTAL OF 182 AWARDS WON, AMONG WHICH ARE SEVERAL TOP 40 AWARDS, BILLBOARD MUSIC AWARDS, AMAS, VMAS, EMAS AND NME AWARDS.

THANK YOU TO THE FANS, EVERYTHING WE DO IS FOR YOU!

NOVEMBER 9, 2012, "TAKE ME HOME" IS THE SECOND STUDIO ALBUM BY BRITISH-IRISH BOY BAND ONE DIRECTION, RELEASED BY SONY MUSIC.

NOVEMBER 25TH, 2013, MIDNIGHT MEMORIES IS THE THIRD STUDIO ALBUM BY BRITISH-IRISH GROUP ONE DIRECTION.

NOVEMBER 17, 2014, "FOUR" IS THE FOURTH STUDIO ALBUM BY THE BRITISH-IRISH GROUP ONE DIRECTION. THE ALBUM HAD A FAVORABLE RECEPTION, DEBUTED AT NO. 1 ON THE US BILLBOARD 200 CHART AND WAS THE SEVENTH BEST-SELLING ALBUM AROUND THE WORLD IN 2014.

"THANKFUL FOR EVERYTHING IN GENERAL...WE GET TO DO THIS AS A JOB...WE ARE VERY LUCKY THAT PEOPLE COME OUT AND SEE US."

FEBRUARY 7, 2015 "ON THE ROAD AGAIN TOUR" WAS THE FOURTH MUSICAL TOUR OF THE BRITISH-IRISH BOY BAND ONE DIRECTION.

MARCH 25TH, 2015, ZAYN MALIK ANNOUNCED HIS DEPARTURE FROM THE BOY BAND ON FACEBOOK. ZAYN MALIK ANNOUNCED HE'D BE LEAVING ONE DIRECTION "TO BE A NORMAL 22-YEAR-OLD," AND, MORE TRUTHFULLY, TO WORK ON HIS OWN SOLO CAREER IN MARCH OF 2015.

"MY LIFE WITH ONE DIRECTION HAS BEEN MORE THAN I COULD EVER HAVE IMAGINED," HE WROTE. "BUT, AFTER FIVE YEARS, I FEEL LIKE IT IS NOW THE RIGHT TIME FOR ME TO LEAVE THE BAND. I'D LIKE TO APOLOGIZE TO THE FANS IF I'VE LET ANYONE DOWN, BUT I HAVE TO DO WHAT FEELS RIGHT IN MY HEART."

NOVEMBER 13, 2015, "MADE IN THE A.M". IS THE FIFTH STUDIO ALBUM BY THE BRITISH-IRISH BOY BAND, ONE DIRECTION, RELEASED BY COLUMBIA RECORDS AND SYCO MUSIC. THE ALBUM IS THE GROUP'S FIRST WITHOUT FORMER BAND MEMBER ZAYN MALIK.

ON THE NIGHT OF SATURDAY, OCTOBER 31, 2015, IT COULD BE SAID THAT IT WAS THE LAST TIME THAT A CROWD GATHERED IN A STADIUM TO SHOUT, "ONE DIRECTION." IT WAS THEIR FINAL CONCERT TOGETHER AS A BAND.

MARCH 3, 2016, THE BRITISH GROUP ONE DIRECTION, CONFIRMED THAT THEY WOULD TAKE A BREAK FROM MARCH 2016, AFTER THE RELEASE OF THEIR NEXT ALBUM.

In March 2017, he announced that his first solo single, "Sign of the Times", would be released on 7 April. The song peaked at number one on the UK Singles Chart and number four on the Billboard Hot 100.

A glam rock-influenced soft rock power ballad, it drew comparisons to the work of David Bowie. Rolling Stone ranked "Sign of the Times" as the best song of 2017.

"Sign of the Times" the music video featured Styles flying and walking on water.

The video won the Brit Award for British Video of the Year presented by The Voice UK stars Olly Murs, Tom Jones and Jennifer Hudson. As Harry was not in attendance do to filming a film, his friend Olly Murs accepted the award for him.

"Harry Styles, "Sign of the Times"!"

STYLES MADE HIS FEATURE FILM DEBUT IN CHRISTOPHER NOLAN'S WAR FILM DUNKIRK, IN JULY 2017, PLAYING A BRITISH SOLDIER NAMED ALEX IN THE DUNKIRK EVACUATION DURING WORLD WAR II. HE APPEARED ALONGSIDE AN ENSEMBLE CAST WHICH INCLUDED FIONN WHITEHEAD, TOM GLYNN-CARNEY, JACK LOWDEN, KENNETH BRANAGH, CILLIAN MURPHY, MARK RYLANCE, AND TOM HARDY.

NOLAN LATER ADMITTED HE WAS UNAWARE OF THE EXTENT OF STYLES' FAME AND THAT HE WAS CAST "BECAUSE HE FIT THE PART WONDERFULLY AND TRULY EARNED A SEAT AT THE TABLE". THE DAILY TELEGRAPH FILM CRITIC ROBBIE COLLIN PRAISED STYLES FOR HIS "BRIGHT, CONVICTED, AND UNEXPECTEDLY NOT-AT-ALL-JARRING PERFORMANCE".

HIS SELF-TITLED DEBUT ALBUM WAS RELEASED IN MAY 2017, WHEREUPON IT DEBUTED AT NUMBER ONE IN SEVERAL COUNTRIES, INCLUDING AUSTRALIA, THE UK AND THE US. THE RECORD WAS INFLUENCED BY 1970S SOFT ROCK.

THE FILM HARRY STYLES: BEHIND THE ALBUM, WHICH DOCUMENTED THE WRITING AND RECORDING PROCESS FOR THE ALBUM, WAS RELEASED IN MAY 2017 EXCLUSIVELY ON APPLE MUSIC.

STYLES EMBARKED ON HIS FIRST HEADLINING CONCERT TOUR, HARRY STYLES: LIVE ON TOUR, FROM SEPTEMBER 2017 THROUGH TO JULY 2018.

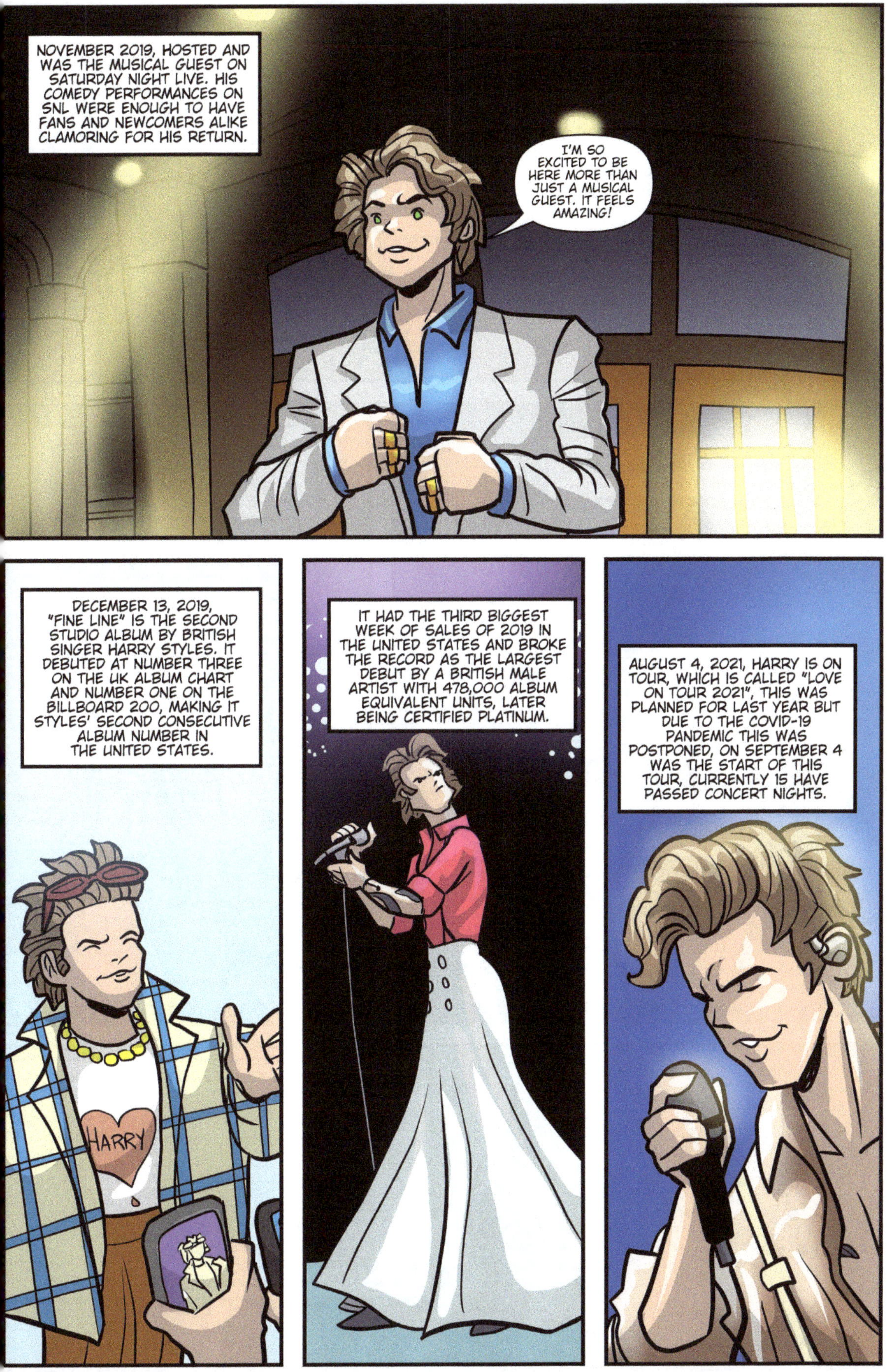

NOVEMBER 2019, HOSTED AND WAS THE MUSICAL GUEST ON SATURDAY NIGHT LIVE. HIS COMEDY PERFORMANCES ON SNL WERE ENOUGH TO HAVE FANS AND NEWCOMERS ALIKE CLAMORING FOR HIS RETURN.

"I'M SO EXCITED TO BE HERE MORE THAN JUST A MUSICAL GUEST. IT FEELS AMAZING!"

DECEMBER 13, 2019, "FINE LINE" IS THE SECOND STUDIO ALBUM BY BRITISH SINGER HARRY STYLES. IT DEBUTED AT NUMBER THREE ON THE UK ALBUM CHART AND NUMBER ONE ON THE BILLBOARD 200, MAKING IT STYLES' SECOND CONSECUTIVE ALBUM NUMBER IN THE UNITED STATES.

IT HAD THE THIRD BIGGEST WEEK OF SALES OF 2019 IN THE UNITED STATES AND BROKE THE RECORD AS THE LARGEST DEBUT BY A BRITISH MALE ARTIST WITH 478,000 ALBUM EQUIVALENT UNITS, LATER BEING CERTIFIED PLATINUM.

AUGUST 4, 2021, HARRY IS ON TOUR, WHICH IS CALLED "LOVE ON TOUR 2021", THIS WAS PLANNED FOR LAST YEAR BUT DUE TO THE COVID-19 PANDEMIC THIS WAS POSTPONED, ON SEPTEMBER 4 WAS THE START OF THIS TOUR, CURRENTLY 15 HAVE PASSED CONCERT NIGHTS.

AT THE 2020 BRIT AWARDS, STYLES WAS NOMINATED FOR BRITISH MALE SOLO ARTIST AND BRITISH ALBUM OF THE YEAR.

HARRY PREFORMED "FALLING" THAT NIGHT ONCE AGAIN BEING THE FASHION ICON.

IN MARCH 2020, HE PERFORMED AN NPR TINY DESK CONCERT, AND IN JULY, HE NARRATED A BEDTIME STORY TITLED DREAM WITH ME FOR THE RELAXATION APP CALM.

STYLES KEEPS WINNING AWARD AFTER AWARD. FAVORITE POP/ROCK ALBUM AWARD FOR "FINE LINE" AT THE 48TH AMERICAN MUSIC AWARDS, THE BEST INTERNATIONAL ARTIST AWARD AT THE 34TH ARIA MUSIC AWARDS, AND THE CHART ACHIEVEMENT AWARD AT THE 27TH BILLBOARDMUSIC AWARDS. HE WAS ALSO NAMED VARIETY'S HITMAKER OF THE YEAR. AT THE 63RD ANNUAL GRAMMY AWARDS IN MARCH 2021, HE RECEIVED THREE NOMINATIONS FOR BEST POP VOCAL ALBUM FOR "FINE LINE", BEST POP SOLO PERFORMANCE "WATERMELON SUGAR" AND BEST MUSIC VIDEO "ADORE YOU", WINNING FOR BEST POP SOLO PERFORMANCE. "WATERMELON SUGAR" ALSO EARNED STYLES HIS SECOND BRIT AWARD FOR BRITISH SINGLE OF THE YEAR DURING THE 2021 CEREMONY.

THE FASHION ICON HARRY STYLES IS THE 1ST SOLO MALE COVER VOGUE. HE WAS DRESSED IN LACE-TRIMMED GUCCI BALLGOWN DRESSED IN A TUXEDO JACKET. STYLES BECOMES AN ICON FOR GENDER-NEUTRAL FASHION.

STYLES BRANCHES OUT INTO MANY DIFFERENT VENTURES. STYLES MADE A CAMEO APPEARANCE AS EROS/STARFOX, BROTHER OF THANOS, IN THE MARVEL CINEMATIC UNIVERSE SUPERHERO FILM ETERNALS, WHICH WAS RELEASED IN NOVEMBER 2021.

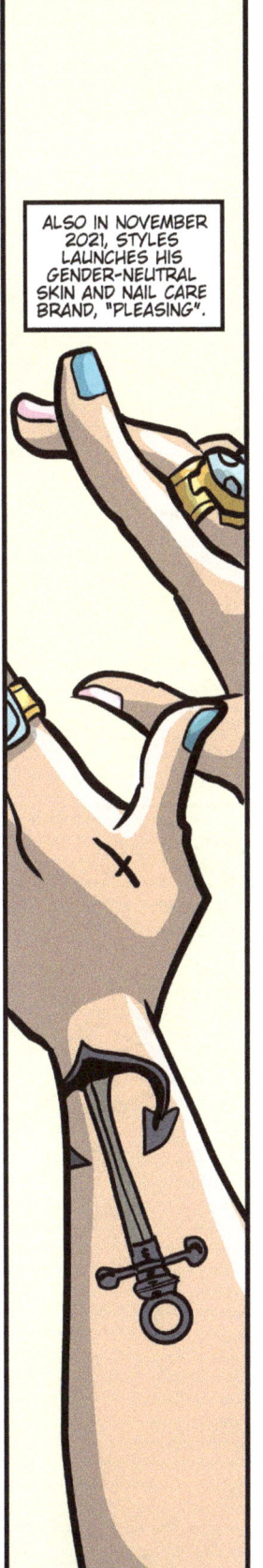

ALSO IN NOVEMBER 2021, STYLES LAUNCHES HIS GENDER-NEUTRAL SKIN AND NAIL CARE BRAND, "PLEASING".

"WHEN WE DECIDED PLEASING WOULD MAKE BEAUTY PRODUCTS, I WANTED TO BE SURE THEY WERE SOMETHING I WOULD USE," STYLES SAID "I DIDN'T WANT TO MAKE PRODUCTS TO MASK PEOPLE, I WANTED TO HIGHLIGHT THEM AND MAKE THEM FEEL BEAUTIFUL."

IN 2022, STYLES ACHIEVED CRITICAL AND COMMERCIAL SUCCESS WITH HIS THIRD ALBUM, HARRY'S HOUSE. ITS LEAD SINGLE "AS IT WAS" DEBUTED ATOP THE UK AND US CHARTS, BECOMING HIS SECOND SOLO NUMBER ONE SINGLE IN BOTH COUNTRIES. IN THE US, IT BECAME THE FOURTH LONGEST RUNNING NUMBER-ONE IN THE CHART'S HISTORY AT 15 WEEKS. THE ALBUM SIMILARLY DEBUTED ATOP THE UK AND US CHARTS.

"THIS FEELS MORE REPRESENTATIVE OF ME AND MY LIFE."

DURING ITS RELEASE WEEK, STYLES OCCUPIED THE TOP SPOT OF THE ALBUM AND SINGLES CHARTS IN BOTH THE UK AND US WITH HARRY'S HOUSE AND "AS IT WAS", RESPECTIVELY. WITH FOUR TRACKS FROM THE ALBUM CONCURRENTLY CHARTING WITHIN THE US TOP 10, HE BECAME THE FIRST BRITISH SOLO ARTIST TO ACHIEVE THIS FEAT.

STYLES' FILM CAREER STARTS TO TAKE OFF. STYLES AUDITIONED FOR THE ROLE OF ELVIS PRESLEY IN BAZ LUHRMANN'S MUSICAL BIOPIC ELVIS. LUHRMANN STATED THAT WHILE "HARRY IS A REALLY TALENTED ACTOR ... THE REAL ISSUE WITH HARRY IS, HE'S HARRY STYLES. HE'S ALREADY AN ICON."

STYLES STARRED ALONGSIDE FLORENCE PUGH IN THE 2022 PSYCHOLOGICAL THRILLER FILM "DON'T WORRY DARLING", DIRECTED BY OLIVIA WILDE. HAVING PREMIERED AT THE 79TH VENICE INTERNATIONAL FILM FESTIVAL.

ALSO IN 2022, STYLES STARRED ALONGSIDE EMMA CORRIN IN "MY POLICEMAN", A FILM ADAPTATION OF THE 2012 NOVEL OF THE SAME NAME WHICH PREMIERED AT THE TORONTO INTERNATIONAL FILM FESTIVAL. AT THE 2022 TIFF TRIBUTE AWARDS, THE MAIN CAST OF THE FILM WERE AWARDED THE TIFF TRIBUTE AWARD FOR PERFORMANCE.

APRIL 2022, HARRY STYLES HEADLINED THE FRIDAY NIGHT OF THE COACHELLA FESTIVAL IN APRIL 2022. HE PERFORMED SOME OF HIS BIGGEST HITS SUCH AS 'ADORE YOU' AND 'WATERMELON SUGAR', ALONG WITH HIS NEW SINGLE 'AS IT WAS'.

MAY 2022, HARRY STYLES RELEASED 'HARRY HOUSE', THE THIRD SOLO ALBUM FROM HIM. HARRY HAS SAID THIS ALBUM "IS THE MOST LIKE ME".

Darren G. Davis — Writer

Ramon Salas — Art

Benjamin Glibert — Letters

Michael Frizell — Editor

Pablo Martinena — Cover

Cover B: Pablo Martinena
Cover C: Ramon Salas
Cover D: Martin Gimenez

Darren G. Davis
Publisher

Maggie Jessup
Publicity

Susan Ferris
Entertainment Manager

Steven Diggs Jr.
Marketing Manager

FAME AND CONTENTS ARE COPYRIGHT © AND ™ DARREN G. DAVIS. ALL RIGHTS RESERVED. TIDALWAVE IS COPYRIGHT © AND ™ DARREN G. DAVIS. ALL RIGHTS RESERVED. ANY REPRODUCTION OF THIS MATERIAL IS STRICTLY PROHIBITED IN ANY MEDIA FORM OTHER THAN FOR PROMOTIONAL PURPOSES UNLESS DARREN G. DAVIS OR TIDALWAVE PUBLISHING GIVES WRITTEN CONSENT. PRINTED IN THE USA
www.tidalwavecomics.com

Ingram Content Group UK Ltd.
Milton Keynes UK
UKHW051016230523
422199UK00003B/35